AMAZE
THEM GOD
WITH

KEVIN DEYOUNG

10 Publishing
a division of **10** of those.com

The content of this book is taken from Don't Call It a Comeback: The
Old Faith for a New Day Copyright © 2011 by Kevin DeYoung

Published by Crossway a publishing ministry of
Good News Publishers Wheaton, Illinois 60187, U.S.A.

This edition published by arrangement with Crossway.
All rights reserved.

Copyright © 2015 by Kevin DeYoung

This edition first published in Great Britain in 2016

Reprinted 2016, 2018 and 2019

British Library Cataloguing in Publication Data
A record for this book is available from the British Library

ISBN: 978-1-910587-54-6

Designed and typeset by Pete Barnsley (Creative Hoot)

Printed and bound in Denmark by Nørhaven

10Publishing, a division of 10ofthose.com
Unit C, Tomlinson Road, Leyland, PR25 2DY, England

Email: info@10ofthose.com
Website: www.10ofthose.com

AMAZE

THEM WITH GOD

KEVIN DEYOUNG

WINNING THE NEXT
GENERATION FOR CHRIST

CONTENTS

HOPE FOR THE FUTURE

My hope is that this little book might be of some small use in reforming God's church according to the Word of God and forming Christians in the truth of God's Word. Contrary to the doom-and-gloom reports, the evangelical church is not dead. By God's grace, no matter the financial, military, or political turmoil we may be called upon to endure, the Western church may have its strongest, healthiest, most vibrant days ahead. Of course, the church will always be "by schisms rent asunder, by heresies distressed," not to mention the problems caused by our own folly and selfishness. But we see signs of renewed interest in the corporate nature of the church, in social engagement, in robust theological commitment, and in a mature, risk-taking, Godsaturated faith that has no patience for gimmicks, imitations, or cultural Christianity. We are sinners, but God is gracious. So the church is bound to be a mixed bag. It is now and will be in the future. For this we can be sorrowful, yet always rejoicing. Sorrowful over suffering, yet always rejoicing in our redemption. Sorrowful for our sins, yet always rejoicing in our Saviour. My prayer is that this book would help a new generation of Christians rejoice in the most important aspects of our faith and walk, instead of sorrowing to discover that we don't know what to think or how to live like Christians.

THE SECRET TO REACHING THE NEXT GENERATION

Getting a book published is a funny thing. People you've never met suddenly think you're amazing. Other people you've never met (who may leave a review on Amazon) think you're the scum of the earth (and not the good Pauline kind). And lots of people expect you to be an expert in things you don't know much about.

After my first book came out, *Why We're Not Emergent*, pastors and other Christians started asking me how my church reached out to young people. "We don't want to go emergent," the questioner would explain. "We need sound doctrine. We need good preaching. But what do you do in your church to reach the next generation?" My usual response was, "Nothing." I wanted people to understand that there's nothing fancy or brilliant about our church strategy. We are just trying to be faithful.

But after a while I began to sense that "nothing" was not a terribly helpful answer. So I talked about our campus ministry, and staff structure, and our small groups—all of which matter. Yet this answer seemed like more of the same. "If you want to reach young people, you have to have this programme or capture this feel or go for this look." Don't get me wrong; thinking about strategy, structure, and feel is not sinful. I'm thankful for all the people in our church who work hard in these areas. I try to be wise in these areas. But this is not the secret to reaching the next generation.

There have been times as a pastor when I've been discouraged by the slowness of numerical growth in my congregation. I've thought, "Why is that church over there so successful? Why did they go from 150 to 1500 in three years?" I've even been borderline snippy at times: "Lord, if I get to heaven and find out there was some secret musical style or movie clip or new programme I was supposed to use in order to be successful, I'm going to feel pretty bummed." But in my saner moments I've come to see two things: (1) It's more my sinful flesh than my sanctified spirit that wants success. And (2) the secret is that there is no secret.

Reaching the next generation—whether they are outside the church or sitting there bored in your church—is easier and harder than you think. It's easier because you don't have to get a degree in postmodern literary theory or go to a bunch of stupid movies. You don't have to say "sweet" or "bling" or know what LOL or IMHO means. You don't have to listen to ... well, whatever people listen to these days. You don't have to be on Twitter, watch the latest box set, or drink fancy coffees. You just have to be like Jesus. That's it. So the easy part is you don't have to be with it. The hard part is you have to be with *him*. If you walk with God and walk with people, you'll reach the next generation.

Let me unpack that a bit. After thinking through the question for over a year, I've come up with five suggestions for pastors, youth workers, campus staff, and anyone else who wants to pass the faith on to the next generation: Grab them with passion. Win them with love. Hold them with holiness. Challenge them with truth. Amaze them with God.

GRAB THEM WITH PASSION

Increasingly, people do not go to church out of a sense of cultural obligation. This is true especially among the young. Newer generations will not give Christianity a second thought if it seems lifeless, repetitive, and uninspiring. They will only get serious about the Christian faith if it seems like something seriously worth their time. You can have formal services, so long as you do not have formalism. You can have casual services, so long as you do not approach your faith casually. Your services can have a lot of different looks, but young people want to see passion. They want to see us do church and follow Christ like we mean it.

We would do well to pay attention to Romans 12. "Let love be genuine. Abhor what is evil; hold fast to what is good. Love one another with brotherly affection. Outdo one another in showing honour. Do not be slothful in zeal, be fervent in spirit, serve the Lord" (vv. 9–11). We would be far less likely to lose our young

PEOPLE NEED TO SEE THAT GOD IS THE ALL CONSUMING REALITY IN OUR LIVES.

people and far more likely to win some others if the spiritual temperature of our churches was something other than lukewarm. People need to see that God is the all-consuming reality in our lives. Our sincerity and earnestness in worship matter ten times more than the style we use to display our sincerity and earnestness.

I'm tired of talking about authenticity, as if prattling on about how messed up you are or blogging about your goldfish are signs of spiritual maturity. We need passion, a zeal fuelled by knowledge (Rom. 10:2). Young people want to see that our faith actually matters to us. They are like Ben Franklin when asked why he was going to hear George Whitefield preach. "You don't even believe what he says," people told Franklin. To which he replied, "I know. But he does." If our evangelical faith is boring to us, it will be boring to others. If the gospel is old news to you, it will be dull news to everyone else.

We cannot pass on what we do not feel. Whitefield blasted the church in his day because "the generality of preachers [in New England] talk of an unknown and unfelt Christ. The reason why congregations have been so dead is

WE CANNOT PASS ON WHAT WE DO NOT FEEL.

because they have had dead men to preach to them."[1] The next generation, every generation really, needs to hear the gospel with personal, passionate pleading. There is a time for dialogue, but there is also a time for declaration. People don't need a lecture or an oration or a discussion from the pulpit on Sunday morning. They need to hear of the mighty deeds of God. And they need to hear the message from someone who not only understands it but has been captured by it.

If we are to grab the next generation with the gospel, we must grab them with passion. And to grab them with passion, we must be gripped with it ourselves. The world needs to see Christians burning, not with self-righteous fury at the sliding morals in our country, but with passion for God. As W. E. Sangster put it, "I'm not interested to know if you could set the Thames on fire. What I want to know is this: if I picked you up by the scruff of your neck and dropped you into the Thames, would it sizzle?"[2]

WIN THEM WITH LOVE

The evangelical church has spent far too much time trying to figure out cultural engagement and far too little time just trying to love. If we listen to people patiently and give them the gift of our curiosity, we will be plenty engaged. I'm not arguing for purposeful obscurantism. What I'm arguing for is getting people's attention with a force more powerful than the right lingo and the right movie clips.

We spend all this time trying to imitate Gen-X culture or Millennial culture, and to what end? For starters, there is no universal youth culture. Young people do not all think alike, dress alike, or feel comfortable in the same environments.

Moreover, even if we could figure out "what the next generation likes," by the time we figured it out they probably wouldn't like it anymore. Count on it: when the church discovers cool, it won't be cool anymore. I've seen well-meaning Christians try to introduce new music into the church in an effort to reach the young people, only to find out that the "new" music included "Shine, Jesus, Shine" and "Shout to the Lord." There's nothing worse than a church trying to be

> THE EVANGELICAL CHURCH NEEDS TO STOP PREACHING THE FALSE GOSPEL OF CULTURAL IDENTIFICATION.

fresh and turning out to be a little dated. Better to stick with the hymns and the organ than do "new" music that hasn't aged terribly well or do the new music in an embarrassing way.

The evangelical church needs to stop preaching the false gospel of cultural identification. Don't spend all your time trying to figure out how to be just like the next generation. Be yourself. Tell them about Jesus. And love them unashamedly. I think a lot of older Christians are desperate to figure out what young people are into because they are too embarrassed to be themselves and too unsure of themselves to simply love the people they are trying to reach.

Jesus said it best: "By this all people will know that you are my disciples, if you have love for one another" (John 13:35). Jesus did not say, "They will know you are my disciples by how attune you are to new trends in youth culture." Or "They will know you are my disciples by the hip atmosphere you create." Give up on relevance, and try love. If they see love in you, love for each other, love for the world, and love for them, they will listen. No matter who "they" are.

Talk to people. Notice visitors. Invite new people over for lunch. Strike up a friendly conversation at the greasy pizza joint. Let your teenagers' friends hang out at your house. Love won't guarantee the young people will never walk away from the church, but it will make it a lot harder. It won't guarantee that non-Christians will come to Christ, but it will make the invitation a whole lot more attractive.

HOLD THEM WITH HOLINESS

Let me make this clear one more time. I'm not arguing that thinking about music styles or paying attention to the "feel" of our church or trying to exegete the culture is sinful stuff. I'm not saying we shouldn't be asking questions related to cultural engagement. What I'm saying is that being experts in the culture matters nothing, and worse than nothing, if we are not first of all experts in love, truth, and holiness.

Look at what God says in 2 Peter 1:5–8:

For this very reason, make every effort to supplement your faith with virtue, and virtue with knowledge, and knowledge with self-control, and self-control with steadfastness, and steadfastness with godliness, and godliness with brotherly affection, and brotherly affection with love. For if these qualities are yours and are increasing, they keep you from being ineffective or unfruitful in the knowledge of our Lord Jesus Christ.

Did you pick up on the promise in the last verse? If we are growing in faith, virtue, knowledge, self-control, steadfastness, godliness, brotherly affection, and love, we will not be ineffective

GROW IN GOD AND YOU'LL MAKE A DIFFERENCE IN PEOPLE'S LIVES.

ministers for Christ. If ever there was a secret to effective ministry, these verses give it to us. Grow in God and you'll make a difference in people's lives. If nothing of spiritual significance is happening in your church, your

Bible study, your small group, or your family, it may be because nothing spiritually significant is happening in your life.

I love the line from Robert Murray M'Cheyne: "My people's greatest need is my personal holiness." I've given that advice to others dozens of times, and I've repeated it to myself

> **"MY PEOPLE'S GREATEST NEED IS MY PERSONAL HOLINESS."**

a hundred times. Almost my whole philosophy of ministry is summed up in M'Cheyne's words. My congregation needs me to be humble before they need me to be smart. They need me to be honest more than they need me to be a dynamic leader. They need me to be teachable more than they need me to teach at conferences. If your walk matches your talk, if your faith costs you something, if being a Christian is more than a cultural garb, they will listen to you.

Paul told young Timothy to keep a close watch on his life and his doctrine (1 Tim. 4:16). "Persist in this," he said, "for by so doing you will save both yourself and your hearers." Far too much ministry today is undertaken without any concern for holiness. We've found that changing the way we do church is easier than changing the way we are. We've found that we are not sufficiently unlike anyone else to garner notice, so we've attempted to become just like everyone else instead. Today's young people do not want a cultural Christianity that fits in like a Baptist church in Texas. They want a conspicuous Christianity that changes lives and transforms communities. Maybe we would make more progress in reaching the next generation if we were making more progress in holiness (1 Tim. 4:15).

Remember, the next generation is not just out there. They are also in here, sitting in our churches week after week. We often hear about how dangerous college can be for Christian teens, how many of them check out of church once they reach the university. But studies have shown that most of the students who check out do so in high school, not in college. It's not liberal professors that are driving our kids away. It's their hard hearts and our stale, compromised witness that opens the door for them to leave.

One of our problems is that we have not done a good job of modelling Christian faith in the home and connecting our youth with other mature Christian adults in the church. One youth leader has commented that how often our young people "attended youth events (including Sunday school and discipleship groups) was not a good predictor of which teens would and which would not grow toward Christian adulthood." Instead,

almost without exception, those young people who are growing in their faith as adults were teenagers who fit into one of two categories: either (1) they came from families where Christian growth was modelled in at least one of their parents, or (2) they had developed such significant connections with adults within the church that it had become an extended family for them.[3]

Likewise, sociologist Christian Smith argues that though most teenagers and parents don't realise it, "a lot of research in the sociology of religion suggests that the most important social influence in shaping young people's religious

THE ONE INDISPENSABLE REQUIREMENT FOR PRODUCING GODLY, MATURE CHRISTIANS IS GODLY, MATURE CHRISTIANS.

lives is the religious life modelled and taught to them by their parents."[4]

The take home from all this is pretty straightforward. The one indispensable requirement for producing godly, mature Christians is godly, mature Christians. Granted, good parents still have wayward children and faithful mentors don't always get through to their pupils. Personal holiness is not the key that regenerates the heart. The Spirit blows where he will. But make no mistake, the promise of 2 Peter 1 is as true as ever. If we are holy, we will

IF WE ARE HOLY, WE WILL BE FRUITFUL.

be fruitful. Personal connections with growing Christians is what the next generation needs more than ever.

CHALLENGE THEM WITH TRUTH

In the church-growth heyday, scholars and pastors were wrestling with how to reach out without dumbing down. Today I would argue that we reach out precisely by *not* dumbing down. The door is open like never before to challenge people with good Bible teaching. People want to learn doctrine. They really do, even non-Christians. Whether they accept it all or not, they want to know what Christians actually believe. Young people will not put up with feel-good pablum. They want the truth straight up, unvarnished, and unashamed.

Thom Rainer did a study a number of years ago asking formerly unchurched people the open-ended question, "What factors led you to choose this church?" A lot of surveys had been done asking the unchurched what they would like in a church. But this study asked the *formerly* unchurched why they actually were now in a church. The results were surprising: 11% said worship style led them to their church, 25% said children's/youth ministry, and 37% said they sensed God's presence at their church. For 41%, someone from the church had witnessed to them, and 49% mentioned friendliness as the reason for choosing their church. Can you guess the top two responses? Doctrine and preaching—88% said the doctrine led them to their church, and 90% said the preaching led them there, in particular, a pastor who preached with certitude and conviction.[5] One woman remarked,

> We attended a lot of different churches for different reasons before we became Christians. I tell you, so many of the preachers spoke with

little authority; they hardly ever dealt with tough issues of Scripture, and they soft-sold the other issues. Frank and I know now that we were hungry for the truth. Why can't preachers learn that shallow and superficial preaching doesn't help anybody, including people like us who weren't Christians.[6]

When it comes to reaching outsiders, bold, deep, biblical preaching is not the problem. It's part of the solution.

The next generation *in* our churches needs to be challenged too. In his book on the religious and spiritual lives of American

> ## THE NEXT GENERATION *IN* OUR CHURCHES NEEDS TO BE CHALLENGED TOO.

teenagers, Christian Smith coined the phrase "Moralistic Therapeutic Deism" to describe the spirituality of American youth. They believe in being a good moral person. They believe religion should give you peace, happiness, and security. They believe God exists and made the world but is not particularly involved in the day-to-day stuff of life.[7] We are naïve if we think this is not the faith of some of the best and brightest in our churches, or even those reading this book!

Church people are not stupid. They are not incapable of learning. For the most part, they simply haven't been taught. No one has challenged them to think a deep thought or read a difficult book. No one has asked them to articulate their faith in biblical and theological categories. We have expected almost nothing out of our young people, so that's what we get.

WE CANNOT CHALLENGE OTHERS UNTIL WE HAVE FIRST CHALLENGED OURSELVES.

A couple of generations ago twenty-year-olds were getting married, starting families, working at real jobs, or off somewhere fighting Nazis.

Today thirty-five-year olds are hanging out on Facebook, looking for direction, and trying to find themselves. We have been coddled when we should have been challenged.

CHALLENGING THE NEXT GENERATION WITH TRUTH STARTS WITH HONEST SELF-EXAMINATION.

Challenging the next generation with truth starts with honest self-examination. We must ask, Do I know the plotline of the Bible? Do I know Christian theology? Do I read any meaty Christian books? Do I know anything about justification, redemption, original sin, propitiation, and progressive sanctification? Do I really understand the gospel? We cannot challenge others until we have first challenged ourselves. That's one of the driving passions behind this book. I want the "average" churchgoer to think more deeply about his faith. I want Christians to realize, like I did that night in college, that they have a lot more to learn.

You've heard it said that Christianity in America is a mile wide and an inch deep. Well, it's more like half a mile wide now. Christian influence is not as pervasive as it once was. I'm convinced that if Christianity is to be a mile wide again in America, it will first have to find a way to be a mile deep. Shallow Christianity will not last in the coming generation, and it will not grow. Cultural Christianity is fading. The church in the twenty-first century must go big on truth or go home.

AMAZE THEM WITH GOD

I beg of you, don't go after the next generation with mere moralism, either on the right (don't have sex, do go to church, share your faith, stay off drugs) or on the left (recycle, dig a well, feed the homeless, buy a wristband). The gospel is not a message about what we need to do for God, but about what God has done for us. So get them with the good news about who God is and what he has done for us.

Some of us, it seems, are almost scared to tell people about God. Perhaps because we don't truly know him. Maybe because we prefer living in triviality. Or maybe because we don't consider knowing God to be very helpful in real life. I have to fight against this unbelief in my own life. If only I would trust God that he is enough to win the hearts and minds of the next generation. It's his work much more than it is mine or yours. So make him front and centre. Don't preach your doubts as mystery. And don't reduce God to your own level. If ever people were starving for a God the size of God, surely it is now.

> ## IF EVER PEOPLE WERE STARVING FOR A GOD THE SIZE OF GOD, SURELY IT IS NOW.

Give them a God who is holy, independent, and unlike us, a God who is good, just, full of wrath, and full of mercy. Give them a God who is sovereign, powerful, tender, and true. Give them a God with edges. Give them an undiluted God who makes them feel cherished and safe, and small and uncomfortable too. Give them a God who works all things after the counsel of his will and for the glory of his name. Give them a God whose love is lavish and free. Give them a God worthy of wonder and fear, a God big enough for all our faith, hope, and love.

Do your friends, your church, your family, your children know that God is the centre of the

> GIVE THEM A GOD WORTHY OF WONDER AND FEAR, A GOD BIG ENOUGH FOR ALL OUR FAITH, HOPE, AND LOVE.

universe? Can they see that he is at the centre of your life?

Imagine you had a dream of someone sitting on a throne. In your dream a rainbow encircled the throne. Twenty-four men surrounded the throne. Lightning and thunder issued from the throne. Seven lamps stood blazing at the foot of the throne. A sea of glass lay before the throne. Four strange creatures were around the throne, giving thanks to him who sits on the throne. And twenty-four dudes were falling down before the one who sits on the throne. You wouldn't have to get Joseph out of prison to figure out the point of this dream. The throne is the figurative and literal centre of the vision. The meaning of the dream is God.

This, of course, is no ordinary dream. It is John's vision from Revelation 4. And it is reality, right now. More substantial and more lasting and more influential than your pain, or fear, or temptation, or opposition, or makeup, or clothes, or boyfriends, or video games, or iPods, or BlackBerrys, or whatever else our culture says should be important to young people is

> AS YOU TRY TO REACH THE NEXT GENERATION FOR CHRIST, YOU CAN AMAZE THEM WITH YOUR CLEVERNESS, YOUR HUMOUR, OR YOUR LOOKS. OR YOU CAN AMAZE THEM WITH GOD.

God. What matters now and for eternity is the unceasing worship of him who sits on the throne.

As you try to reach the next generation for Christ, you can amaze them with your cleverness, your humour, or your looks. Or you can amaze them with God. I need a lot of things in my life. There are schedules and details and a long to-do list. I need food and water and shelter.

... THIS IS MY GREATEST NEED AND YOURS: TO KNOW GOD, LOVE GOD, DELIGHT IN GOD, AND MAKE MUCH OF GOD.

I need sleep. I need more exercise, and I need to eat better. But this is my greatest need and yours: to know God, love God, delight in God, and make much of God.

We have an incredible opportunity before us. Most people live weightless, ephemeral lives. We can give them substance instead of style. We can show them a big God to help make sense of their shrinking lives. We can point them to transcendence instead of triviality. We can reach them with something more lasting and more powerful than gimmicks, gadgets, and games. We can reach them with God.

Imagine that. Reaching the next generation *for* God by showing them *more* of God. That's just crazy enough to work.

FOR FURTHER READING

This book is taken from *Don't Call It a Comeback*: Crossway, 2011

NOTES

1. Roger Finke and Rodney Stark, *The Churching of America, 1776–2005* (Piscataway, NJ: Rutgers University Press, 2005), 53.

2. Quoted in John R. W. Stott, *Between Two Worlds: The Challenge of Preaching Today* (Grand Rapids: Eerdmans, 1982), 285.

3. Mark DeVries, *Family-Based Youth Ministry: Reaching the Been-There, Done-That Generation* (Downers Grove, IL: InterVarsity, 1994), 63.

4. Christian Smith, with Melissa Lundquist Denton, *Soul Searching: The Religious and Spiritual Lives of American Teenagers* (New York: Oxford University Press, 2005), 56.

5. Thom Rainer, *Surprising Insights from the Unchurched* (Grand Rapids: Zondervan, 2001), 74.

6. Ibid., 62.

7. Smith and Denton, *Soul Searching*, 162ff.

a division of **10** of those.com